ARCHBISHOP FULTON J. SHEEN

A Man for All Media

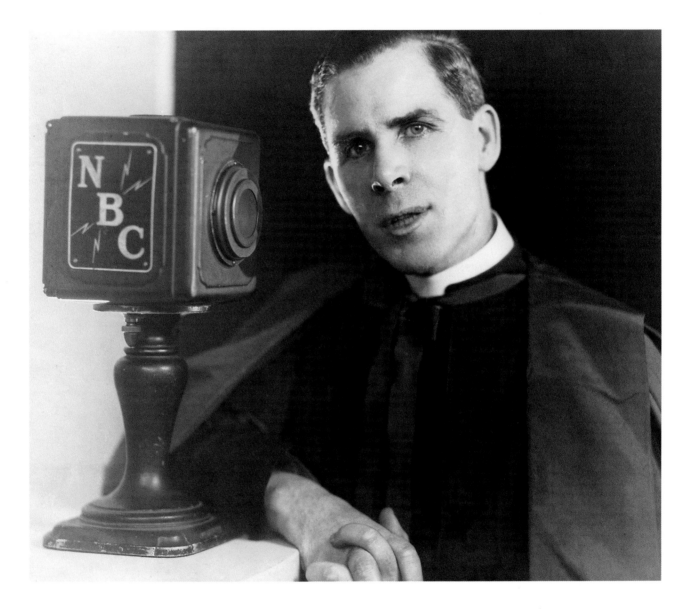

ARCHBISHOP FULTON J. SHEEN

A Man for All Media

DA PER MATREM ME VENIRE

GREGORY JOSEPH LADD

IGNATIUS PRESS   SAN FRANCISCO

**The Coat of Arms of
Archbishop Fulton John Sheen**

The arms of archbishops, both residential
and titular, consist of a shield or personal
armorial device of the prelate placed upon
the archiepiscopal cross (represented by
two horizontal bars). Above the
archiepiscopal cross is the *galero* (hat) of
green with two green *fiocchi* at the brim
and ten green *fiocci* suspended from green
cords on either side of the shield. The coat
of arms of the Sheen family of Ireland
displays a dove holding an olive branch in
its beak, as canting arms for the surname.
Canting arms herald or "sing out" the
name of the bearer. *Sheen* in Gaelic means
"peaceful". The arms bear a golden globe
of the earth to denote his office as National
Director of the Society for the Propagation
of the Faith. The Latin motto translates:
"Grant that I may come to Thee through
Thy Mother."

Photographs and quotations
© The Fulton J. Sheen Foundation
Photograph credits appear on page 144.

Cover design by Christopher J. Pelicano

ISBN 0–89870–853–2
Library of Congress control number 200091147

Printed in China by C&C Printing Co., Ltd.

"Believe the incredible, and you can do the impossible. It is our want of faith that holds us back, even as Peter. When did he begin to sink? The Gospel gives us the reason. He took account of the winds, he began reading some surveys; it was established statistically that 99.44 percent of mankind cannot walk on water. All of the incredulities were in the winds. When he took his eyes off Christ, Peter began to sink."

—FULTON J. SHEEN

ACKNOWLEDGMENTS

Thanks be to Almighty God and to those who helped make this book of photographs and quotations a reality at a time when great words of wisdom are needed to "fuel" the spirit with God's eternal hope. My gratitude goes particularly to:

Most Reverend Matthew H. Clark, Bishop of the Diocese of Rochester, New York; Sister Patricia Schoelles, S.S.J., President of Saint Bernard's Institute; Linda Barton, Secretary of the Institute; Sebastian Falcone; Greg Francis, photographer; Sister Connie Derby; and Father William Graf of the Archives of the Diocese of Rochester.

The Society for the Propagation of the Faith; Reverend Albert Mary Shamon, Vicar of Education in the Diocese of Rochester during the term of Archbishop Sheen; the Viatorian Fathers of Arlington Heights, Illinois; the town of El Paso, Illinois, and its residents; the relatives of Archbishop Sheen, including Joan Fulton Kapraun, Merle Fulton, and Miles and Dee Cleary.

Also my attorney Ted Burzynski; Karen Fulte and Jane Peverly of the Sheen Foundation, El Paso, Illinois; Janet Newlin, archivist of the Archdiocese of Indianapolis, Indiana; Lawrence and Jean Hickey of New York City; Oscar Delgado of Chicago; Most Reverend John J. Myers, Bishop of the Diocese of Peoria, Illinois (Archbishop Sheen's home diocese); Francis Cardinal George, O.M.I., Archbishop of Chicago; the late John Cardinal O'Connor; and Reverend Andrew Apostoli, C.F.R., spiritual advisor for the Sheen Foundation.

My thanks are due also to Edda Taylor, photographer; to my associate editor and longtime friend David C. Solan, whose support and talent helped bring this work to fulfillment; to Reverend Joseph Fessio, S.J., editor of Ignatius Press; to Christopher J. Pelicano, Roxanne Mei Lum, and Paul and Joan Zomberg for their assistance in the design and production of this book; and, of course, to my family, especially my mother, who has been born into eternity, and my father. *Deo gratias!*

G. J. L.

PREFACE

In 1999, an Internet website known as the *Daily Catholic* conducted a survey over a three-month period to determine the "Top 100 Catholics of the Twentieth Century". The response totaled 23,455 votes, nominating 728 candidates. Granted, this was not the most scientific approach to such a survey, yet its results are informative.

The top three choices, I am sure, would not come as a surprise to anyone today. First was Pope John Paul II, who ranks in his own lifetime among the most holy and influential popes in the history of the Catholic Church. Second was Mother Teresa of Calcutta, the "saint of the gutters" and foundress of the Missionaries of Charity. Her marvelous work among the poorest of the poor won her the admiration and affection of many all over the world. The third place was given to Bl. Padre Pio of Pietrelcina, the great Capuchin Franciscan priest and mystic, who bore the wounds of Jesus Christ in his hands, feet, and side for fifty years of his life.

The fourth-highest in the list, however, might come as a surprise to some Catholics. It was Archbishop Fulton J. Sheen, the Catholic Church's first great "televangelist", who profoundly touched the lives of millions, Catholics and non-Catholics alike, through radio, television, and the written word. This evidence of his standing among those who submitted their list of names is surprising in that Archbishop Sheen was regarded as more influential than four popes—Pius X, Pius XII, Paul VI, and John XXIII—and three saints—St. Faustina Kowalska, St. Maximilian Kolbe, and St. Teresa Benedicta of the Cross (Edith Stein). What does this tell us? It is clear that in the estimation of many Catholics, Archbishop Sheen ranks among the very "giants" of their Faith.

His inspiring effect on people is hard to describe, because it may easily seem, especially to those who did not know him when he was alive, that it is now being exaggerated. I was one of the estimated thirty million people who, every Tuesday evening for seven years, watched his award-winning television series *Life Is Worth Living*. Never did I think I would ever meet this truly remarkable man. However, by God's Providence, I not only met him, but I was ordained a priest forever by him on March 16, 1967! By both his example and his teachings, he helped me to realize what goes into making a faithful priest.

Recently, there has been a noticeable revival of Archbishop Sheen's popularity. His message is once again being shared, thanks to a renewed interest in his books and video and audio recordings. His message has always had a certain "timelessness" to it, because it is rooted in Christ, who is "the same yesterday, today and always" (Heb 13:8). Many people have told me that when they read the Archbishop's writings or listen to his recorded words, he could easily be taken as talking about our situation today, right now. There is a truly "prophetic" quality to his message.

In that message, two words stand out for me as very significant. The first is "love", the word he always left us with. Whether he was closing a TV show, a talk in a cathedral or chapel, or one of his many letters, almost invariably came the beautiful words, "God love you!" How much we need to hear those words over and over today! In our world, secularized, filled with hatred, violence, and division, we need the love of God to obtain love and peace for our own hearts, and then to share it with our brothers and sisters so that we may all become one in Christ.

Another key word that I associate closely with Archbishop Sheen is "life"! Its importance for him can be seen in the very title he gave to his great TV series, *Life Is Worth Living*. As with the word *love*, we need to hear the word *life* more and more every day! Our times, in the words of Pope John Paul II, are characterized by a fierce struggle between the "culture of life" and the "culture of death". The disregard for the sanctity of human life is evident all around us today. The Archbishop was an early and strong defender of human life in all its stages, from conception to natural death, and in all circumstances.

This book is a very welcome addition to all that has been written about Archbishop Sheen. I have known Gregory Ladd for some time now, and his deep personal love and dedication to the late Archbishop are evident in these pages. Combining pictures of Sheen as child and youth, priest and archbishop, with quotations from the large archive of speeches and writings, he helps us to recognize this great Churchman's enormous contribution to clear thinking about eternal truths. I am sure that all who study this book will be struck by a sense of the sanctity and learning, compassion and humor, that were beautifully blended in the life and timeless message of Archbishop Fulton J. Sheen.

Fr. Andrew Apostoli, C.F.R.

The most profound impact that Archbishop Sheen had was by way of his focus on the theme: *What the world needs is not a voice that is right when the world is right, but a voice that is right when the world is wrong.* May all of us who share his love for the Church share also his willingness to stand as the counter-culture in this very needy world.

+ JOHN CARDINAL O'CONNOR
THE LATE ARCHBISHOP OF NEW YORK

Archbishop Fulton Sheen served the Church in many capacities with great distinction for six decades. Through his faith-filled vision and charming wit, he was able to touch the hearts and inspire the minds of millions. He had a knack for expressing the truths of the Gospel in a compelling way— offering faith, hope, and love to all seeking spiritual enrichment.

+ FRANCIS CARDINAL GEORGE, O.M.I.
ARCHBISHOP OF CHICAGO

Archbishop Sheen was truly a spiritual giant and, in my view, the greatest religious communicator of the twentieth century. He was a person of deep prayer and learning, and he was a compelling speaker who brought the message of Jesus Christ and His Church to millions of people around the world through his columns and books, but especially through his radio and television broadcasts.

+ MOST REVEREND JOHN P. FOLEY
TITULAR ARCHBISHOP OF NEAPOLIS
PONTIFICAL COUNCIL FOR SOCIAL COMMUNICATIONS

Like many Americans, I watched Archbishop Sheen's *Life Is Worth Living* on television in the 1950s. His sparkling wit and dramatic flair were very attractive. But what attracted people even more was his willingness to take on contemporary culture with its presuppositions and to discuss them in the light of the gospel and in the light of sound philosophical principles. People of all faiths and no faith were attracted both by his personality and by his presentation, and even more by the perceptive insight evident in his teaching.

+ MOST REVEREND JOHN J. MYERS
BISHOP OF PEORIA

As pastor of the Crystal Cathedral, I have had the privilege of meeting some of the greatest minds of the twentieth century. One of those great minds belonged to Archbishop Fulton J. Sheen, whom I greatly admired. God gave us a gift when He gave us Archbishop Sheen.

REVEREND ROBERT H. SCHULLER
THE CRYSTAL CATHEDRAL

Jesus was never off the Cross!
As the atom reflects the solar system,
So Bethlehem was the cameo of Calvary.

Once elderly Simeon spoke of His Death
Mary saw the shadow of nails in the Child's hands.

An unsuffering Christ would be a Professor of Ethics.
The Three Temptations were three short-cuts from the Cross:
"Feed the Hungry"—Be a sociological Christ.
"Do breath-taking wonders"—Be a scientific Christ.
"Be a social revolutionist"—Be a Communist Christ.

So long as men wear scars
The imprints of a night forever past
Will trumpet:

MY PAIN! MY SCARS! MY DEATH!

To
My Dear Parents
In Souvenir of
The Honorary Professorship
of their son.
Fulton John.
at.
The University of Louvain.
July 16, 1925.

"When the hand of death is laid upon those whom you love and your heart seems torn in two, climb to the Hill of Calvary to be consoled by the Mother of Sorrows who is also the Cause of Our Joy."

"Beauty on the outside never gets into the soul, but beauty of the soul reflects itself on the face."

"There is no such thing as understanding art in any period apart from the philosophy of that period. Philosophy inspires art and art reflects philosophy. We can never tell what is the art of an age, unless we know what is the thought of that age. If the thought is lofty and spiritual, art will be lofty and spiritual; if thought is base and material, art will be base and material. If the thought is of the heaven heavenly, art will be of the heaven heavenly; if the thought is of the earth earthly, art will be of the earth earthly.".

— From "The Philosophy of Medieval Art", May 28, 1926.

"Not by dying alone, not by experience, but by suffering. Suffering is the great river of wisdom. If one wants counsel, the best one to go to is either a saint or someone who is suffering."

"Which stands up better in a crisis—man or woman? One can discuss this in a series of historical crises, but without arriving at any decision. The best way to arrive at a conclusion is to go to the greatest crisis the world ever faced, namely, the Crucifixion of Our Divine Lord. When we come to this great drama of Calvary, there is one fact that stands out very clearly: men failed. . . . On the other hand, there is not a single instance of a woman's failing Him."

Monsignor Sheen at ground-breaking ceremonies for the Blessed Martin de Porres Hospital for Mothers and Children in Mobile, Alabama.

"Meditation is a more advanced spiritual act than 'saying prayers'. It may be likened to the attitude of a child who breaks into the presence of a mother saying: 'I'll not say a word, if you will just let me stay here and watch you.' Or, as a soldier once told the Curé of Ars: 'I just stand here before the tabernacle; He looks at me and I look at Him.'"

Bishop Sheen talking with Mary Feeley (Kelly), who lived in the house where his grandmother had been born, in Roscommon, Ireland.

A photo taken at Radio City Studios during a broadcast of Monsignor Sheen's NBC radio show The Catholic Hour, *1930s.*

"Forgiveness meets us
more than halfway.
The Kiss of Welcome
is extended before
one work of
penitence or request
had been spoken."

"The Beatitudes represent the divine way to be happy..."

*The senior graduation of Fulton J. Sheen from
Saint Viator College in 1917.*

TOP: *The eighth-grade graduation class of Saint Mary's School in Peoria, c. 1909. Fulton is seated on the floor between the two girls.*
BOTTOM: *The 1914–1915 "affirmative" debate team at Saint Viator College, from the Viatorian yearbook. Left to right: Dan T. Sullivan, Charles Hart, and Fulton J. Sheen.*

THIRD RETREAT OF PRIESTS OF DIOCESE OF RENO NEV.

"I expect the Congress [on Religious Life] to help restore respect for the magisterium of the Church among the religious. This is the basic problem, which is a problem of faith. . . . Either religious recognize the authority of the Church or they follow the anonymous authority or current phraseology, of 'they say' or being 'with it'. . . . The spiritual turmoil among the religious is due to a decline in prayer and neglect of the Cross."

—From a speech on religious life, 1978.

"Saints are impractical; artists and philosophers are impractical. The world has room for only the practical."

"It has not often been discovered how women act in crises, but Mrs. Irene Dunne Griffin is one woman who has not and will not fail in a crisis."

Monsignor Sheen gave the address at the University of Notre Dame, South Bend, Indiana, when the actress Irene Dunne Griffin was awarded the Laetare Medal as the annual recipient in 1949, on June 29.

"I sometimes wish that the charming Mrs. Griffin would reveal her true age, so that I might tell at what age women are most beautiful."

Bishop Sheen in Kenya with that country's first bishop, Maurice Ottunga, later Cardinal Archbishop of Nairobi. Bishop Sheen served as Director for the Society for the Propagation of the Faith from 1950 to 1966.

"Charity embraces within its scope both what we are and what we have. It was to both these Our Divine Lord referred in His Words to the young man: 'Go sell all thou hast'—what you have, 'then come follow Me'—what you are."

—Address to the Ladies of Charity at their annual meeting on Saturday, May 5, 1928, Hotel Plaza, New York City.

SANCTITY

Sanctity, then, is not giving up the world. It is exchanging the world. It is a continuation of that sublime transaction of the Incarnation in which Christ said to Man: *"You give Me your humanity, I will give you My Divinity. You give Me your time, I will give you My eternity. You give Me your bonds, I will give you My Omnipotence. You give Me your slavery, I will give you My freedom. You give Me your death, I will give you My Life. You give Me your nothingness, I will give you My All."* And the consoling thought throughout this whole transforming process is that it does not require much time to make us saints; it requires only much love.

"There is hope for each. . . . Every man is made to the image and likeness of God."

"Every man is on a cross. Some ask to be taken down like the thief on the left; others ask to be taken up like the thief on the right."

"The cross is not something that *has* happened; the Crucifixion is something that *is* happening. It can be found at any place and at any hour in the human race."

"The rabbis and priests and ministers stopped talking about sin. The jurists picked it up and turned sin into a crime, and finally psychiatrists converted it into a complex. The result is that no one is a sinner."

"He will spread the lie that men will never be better until they make society better and thus have selfishness to provide fuel for the next revolution; he will foster science, but only to have armament makers use one marvel of science to destroy another; he will foster more divorces under the guise that one partner is 'vital'. He will increase love for love and decrease love for person; he will invoke religion to destroy religion; he will even speak of Christ and say that he was the greatest *man* who ever lived; he will say his mission is to liberate men from the servitude of superstition and Fascism; he will organize children's games, tell people whom they should and should not marry and unmarry, who should bear children and who should not; he will benevolently draw chocolate bars from his pockets for the little ones, and bottles of milk for the Hottentots."

—From "The Devil according to Archbishop Sheen", *Communism and the Conscience of the West* (1948).

42

"Civilization must recognize the authority of God as a necessary condition in the solution of its ills. The world's experiments with liberty should by this time have taught men that true liberty does not mean the right to violate the laws of God."

—From an article published in the late 1930s.

Bishop Sheen attended many a social function and was a sought-after guest. Here he was the guest of honor at the annual Friars Club roast, October 13, 1973.

FROM LEFT: *Milton Wrightman, Steve Lawrence, Red Buttons, Allen King, Fulton J. Sheen, Milton Berle, Henny Youngman, Jack Benny, Jan Murray, and Don Drysdale.*

Bishop Sheen officiating at Habsburg family wedding in Tuxedo Park, New York, 1953.

"There are only two classes of people in the world: those who are afraid to find God, and those who are afraid to lose God. Some are afraid to find God lest in finding Him they lose their selfish desires, believing all the while that if they had Him they could have naught else besides. Others are afraid to lose God because in losing Him they would lose all there is, and find in return only their petty selves which are so useless for giving true and lasting happiness."

—From a sermon at the Church of the Blessed Sacrament, New York City, on October 26, 1931. On this occasion, a close friend of Father Sheen's was entering the convent of the Sisters of the Poor Clares.

"Maybe our refusal to exercise our body could atrophy our muscles. Could the great increase of heart trouble be due to the fact that few exercise their hearts by hard exercise? I wonder if a ditchdigger ever developed angina pectoris? Maybe it is good for us that at our office and home we have to climb four flights of stairs for every meal."

The Washington, D.C., residence of Monsignor Sheen at the time he was teaching at The Catholic University of America. The decor was Art Deco, as seen in the living room and private chapel.

WITHOUT ME . . . NOTHING

Light is not in the eye, but the eye sees because of it; food is not in the stomach, but it is thanks to food that the body lives; sound is not in the ear, but it is thanks to harmony that the ear hears. In the spiritual order it is the same: what air is to the lungs, prayer is to the soul. As Our Lord said, "Without Me, you can do nothing." He did not mean that we could do nothing in the natural order without Him, but He meant that we could do nothing in the spiritual order without His grace.

Bishop Sheen and Pope Pius XII with Monsignor Edward O'Meara, who succeeded Sheen as Director of the Society for the Propagation of the Faith and later was named Archbishop of the Indianapolis, Indiana, Archdiocese.

Bishop Sheen with Pope John XXIII.

RESTORATION
BY THE DIVINE ARTIST

If you know that you could be better then you are; if you feel like the master painting of a great artist that has become somewhat defaced and stained; if you know that though you are too good for the rubbish heap, you are nevertheless too spoiled to hang in the Metropolitan Gallery; if you know that you cannot restore yourself to your pristine beauty; if you know that no one could restore you better than the Divine Artist who made you—then you have already taken the first step toward peace. The Divine Artist did come to restore the original, and He came on Christmas Day.

"Because Our Lord willed her to us as Our Mother, He left her on this earth after He ascended into heaven, in order that she might mother the infant Church. The infant Church had need of a mother, just as did the infant Christ. She had to remain on earth until her family had grown. That is why we find her on Pentecost abiding in prayer with the Apostles, awaiting the descent of the Holy Spirit. She was mothering the Mystical Body of Christ."

—From a radio address on *The Catholic Hour*, 1936.

"Christianity, because it is outside the civilizations of the East and West, is alone capable of uniting both. Western civilization is practical. In it man does everything. God does nothing. . . . Eastern civilization is mystical. God does everything, man does nothing. . . . Because of its position, Christianity alone is capable of building "One World" by serving as a mediator between both, as it mediates man and the universe, this world and the next."

BOTTOM: *Bishop Sheen with Bishop Nicholas T. Elko, Apostolic Exarch of the Pittsburgh Greek Rite Diocese, and Bishop Emmet M. Walsh of Youngstown, Ohio.*

Archbishop Sheen being welcomed upon his arrival at Sligo, Ireland, in August 1972.

"The shepherd, when he finds the lost sheep, puts it upon his shoulders and rejoices."

Father Sheen (left) during the youthful days of his priesthood at the University of Louvain, in Belgium, during the early 1920s.

"There is a world of difference between what we need and what we want. We need those things which are essential for a normal, comfortable human existence. But we want more than that. Our needs are quickly satisfied, but our wants rarely."

—From a radio broadcast on *The Catholic Hour* in the 1930s.

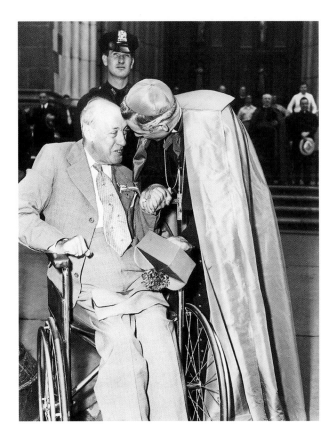 

"There are no plains in the spiritual life; we are either going uphill or coming down."

LEFT: *Bishop Sheen talks with World War I veteran Michael Tressy at the American Legion Parade in New York City, in front of Saint Patrick's Cathedral.*

RIGHT: *Bishop Sheen arrives at the Rochester airport and is greeted by members of his diocese; the next day, December 15, 1966, he was installed as the bishop of the Diocese of Rochester, New York.*

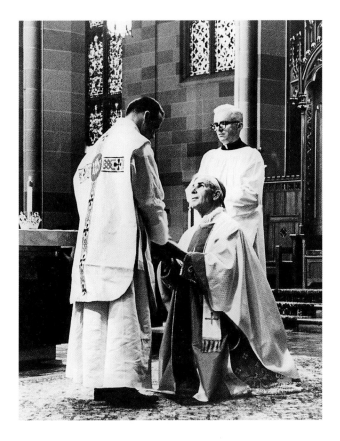 

"If you want to know about God, there is only one way to do it: get down on your knees."

LEFT: *Bishop Sheen receiving the blessing of a newly ordained priest, who was one of those ordained during the years when the Bishop was head of the Diocese of Rochester, New York.*
RIGHT: *The Bishop in quiet meditation before the Blessed Sacrament, where he spent an hour each day and where many of his thoughts and writings originated.*

On June 11, 1951, in the Church of Saints John and Paul (the titular church in Rome of Francis Cardinal Spellman of New York), Monsignor Sheen was consecrated auxiliary bishop for the Archdiocese of New York.

At the conclusion of the ceremony of consecration, Bishop Sheen bestows his first episcopal blessing upon all present.

"Saints have a sense of humor. I do not mean only canonized saints, but rather that great army of staunch and solid Christians to whom everything and every incident speaks a story of God's love. A saint can be defined as one who has a divine sense of humor, for a saint never takes this world seriously as the lasting city."

"The man who thinks only of himself says prayers of petition; he who thinks of his neighbor says prayers of intercession; he who thinks of loving and serving God says prayers of abandonment to God's will, and that is the prayer of the saints."

LEFT: *Fulton John Sheen with his grandfather.*
RIGHT: *The Bishop with his brothers, Albert (left) and Thomas.*

"Clay has to be molded, and that is done primarily in the family, which is more sacred than the state."

Thomas Sheen, M.D., brother of Bishop Sheen, with his wife, Eileen, and their children (August 1947).

"How can we develop leadership if religion abdicates its mission of
uprooting evil from the heart and links itself up either with those who
find evil in the right or in the left. Evil is in the center; in the core of one's
being; in the heart. Until the churches get back to the Cross, to the
training of the will, to the revival of discipline, to the looking into the
heart of the protester, the nation will have an abortion rather than a
rebirth."

—From a newspaper column by Bishop Sheen.

"Mr. President, Mrs. Carter, my fellow sinners . . ."

TOP: *Archbishop Sheen speaks at the National Prayer Breakfast in Washington, D.C., on January 25, 1979. Seated at far left is the Reverend Billy Graham, for whom the Archbishop had deep respect and admiration.*
BOTTOM: *Reverend Billy Graham in conversation with Archbishop Sheen before the National Prayer Breakfast.*

A large poster announcing that Monsignor Sheen was to be the keynote speaker at the Loyola University Forum.

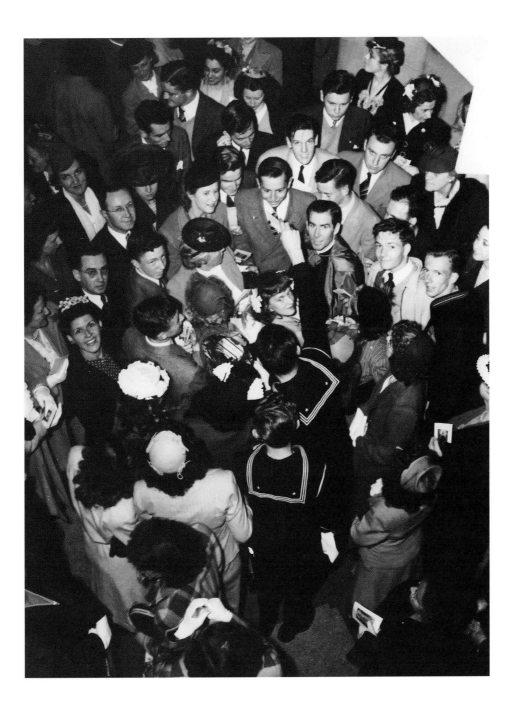

Monsignor Sheen surrounded by a crowd in Providence, Rhode Island, in 1944.

"It used to be that the Catholics were the only ones to believe in the Immaculate Conception; now everyone believes he is immaculately conceived."

TOP: *Monsignor Sheen and Australian welcomers during his 1948 trip.*
LEFT: *Cardinal Spellman and Monsignor Sheen, accompanied by Archbishop Mannise and Cardinal Gilroy, arrive for the Centenary Reception at Xavier College, Melbourne.*
RIGHT: *Monsignor Sheen addressed a crown of forty-five thousand in Melbourne on May 2, 1948.*

WE CANNOT MAKE THE BEST OF TWO WORLDS

"*Fear ye not them that kill the body . . . but rather fear him that can destroy both soul and body in hell.* Calvary is wrapped up in these words of our Blessed Lord, for therein is revealed the supreme struggle of every life—the struggle to preserve our spiritual freedom. We cannot serve both God and Mammon; we cannot save our life both for time and for eternity; we cannot feast both here and hereafter; we cannot make the best of two worlds; either we will have the fast on earth and the feast in heaven, or we will have the feast here and the fast in eternity."

"It is not enough merely to have an intellectual understanding of another man's difficulty; we need to go a little farther to feel it as our own burden."

"Hope is not optimism; it is something born in defeat, agonized amidst anxieties, and yet never giving up because one day a Judge Who sentenced me justly for my crimes came down from the bench, paid my debts as if they were His own, and then took me to Himself. Somewhere, somehow in history is hidden the mystery of love."

—From a newspaper column by Bishop Sheen.

"Hate is mortal because it seeks the death of enemies, and because it has no other badge of victory than a battlefield strewn with the victims of its violence. How could it be otherwise, for how could that which lives by death escape death?"

—From a series of Holy Week sermons published as newspaper columns in 1939.

Bishop Sheen addressing members of the Temple B'Rith Kodesh in Rochester, New York.

LEFT: *Bishop Sheen with Rev. Robert Schuller, pastor and founder of the Crystal Cathedral in Garden Grove, California. Reverend Schuller invited the Bishop to speak to his congregation. A bronze statue of Bishop Sheen has been placed in the Cathedral's Robert Schuller Center, honoring him as one of the few great religious orators of our time.*

RIGHT: *The interior of the Crystal Cathedral on the day when Bishop Sheen spoke to the congregation. He and Reverend Schuller are seated in the upper right balcony during opening ceremonies.*

"There is often a conspiracy in every man against himself; he hunts for excuses to cover up his disobedience, but in a single moment, life can be changed, not by pulling oneself up through the power of his own will, but by a response to Heaven's inspirations which leaves the deserts of the world behind."

—From a newspaper column by Bishop Sheen.

"There is just one point where broadcasting and television must admit their inadequacy and bow down to the fullness of theology, and that is in their incapacity to communicate the final intimacy of affection, touch. Broadcasting and television must be denied this highest kind of personal communication because the radio waves are light waves and not heat waves; they are like to the cold rays of the sun, the ultra-violet, but not like the hot, infrared rays. They can communicate truth but not warmth; knowledge but not love. Anyone may hear us or see us, but few may touch us. That is the privilege of the elect. Religion gives that third degree of intimacy thanks to Communion, wherein Christ and man are one in the unity of spirit. But broadcasting and television must forever be denied that greatest joy of all."

—From the first television broadcast given by Bishop Sheen, in 1951. His inspirational *Life Is Worth Living* was the first prime-time religious television program.

"The most tragic words ever written of Our Lord were those which John sets down in the beginning of his Gospel: He came unto his own, and his own received him not. Bethlehem had no room for Him when He was born; Nazareth, no room for Him when He lived; and Jerusalem, no room for Him when He died."

—From a 1934 radio address titled "Gamblers of Calvary".

"John XXIII, in the name of the sacred united humanity, stretched out his great arms, like the fleshy columns of Bernini, and on the day of his coronation, he bade all mankind to come to his door. Whatever was prejudicial to race or people he eliminated; to his chambers came Buddhists, Communists, Moslems, simply because they were men, and they lived in the world. As a workman at Saint Peter's said of him, 'He doesn't care about politics, except insofar as it affects people like me.' In his *Pacem in Terris*, he wrote: 'One must never confuse error and the person who errs, not even when there is a question of inadequate knowledge of truth in the moral and religious field.' "

—From a newspaper column by Bishop Sheen

Bishop Sheen with Pope John XXIII.

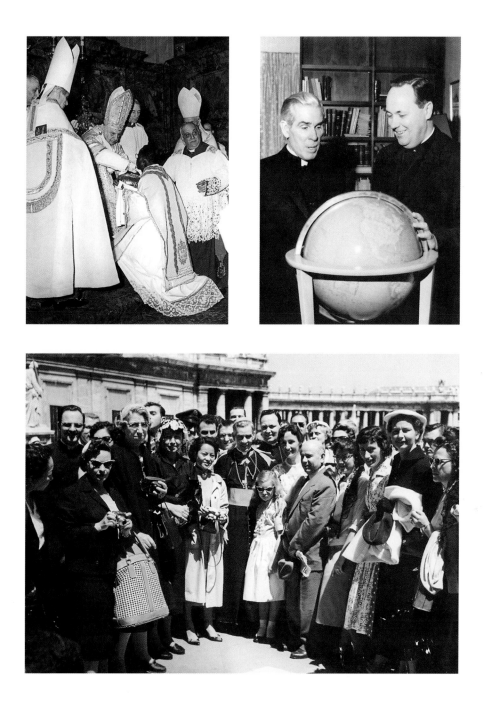

TOP LEFT: *Bishop Sheen as a co-consecrator for missionary bishops, with Pope John XXIII in Rome.*
TOP RIGHT: *Bishop Sheen with Bishop Edward O'Meara, who succeeded him as Director for the Society for the Propagation of the Faith. Bishop O'Meara— who delivered the homily for Bishop Sheen's funeral at Saint Patrick's Cathedral—was later named Archbishop of Indianapolis, Indiana.*
BOTTOM: *Bishop Sheen with a tour group in Rome.*

"Only the mind which humbles itself before the truth it wishes to impart can pass the knowledge on to other minds. The world has never known a humbler teacher than the Word of God Himself, who taught in simple parables and homely examples drawn from sheep and goats and lilies of the field, from patches on worn clothing and wine in new bottles."

Bishop Sheen being interviewed by Hugh Downs during the early 1970s.

Fulton John Sheen as seen in the 1917 Viatorian *yearbook from Saint Viator College in Kankakee, Illinois, where the young man from Peoria was nicknamed "Fult" and "F.J."*

Bishop Fulton J. Sheen, newly installed as bishop of Rochester, New York, in 1966, exchanges the kiss of peace with fourteen-year-old George Mitchell, a representative of the diocese.

"A system of education that completely neglects religion and morality, that trains only the intellect and neglects entirely the will—that system is not worth saving and should be allowed to perish."

—From an address at Loyola College, sponsored by the Loyola Alumni Ladies Auxiliary, in 1938 or 1939.

LOVE WITHOUT LUST

"The Virgin conceived Our Lord without the lust of the flesh, so she brought forth Him in joy without the labor of the flesh. As a bee draws honey from the flower without offending it, as Eve was taken out of the side of Adam without any grief to him, so now in remaking the human race, the new Adam, Christ, is taken from the new Eve, Mary, without any sorrow to her. As our minds beget a thought without in any way destroying the mind, so Mary begot the Word of God without in herself in any way affecting her virginity. In flesh-love the ecstasy is first in the body, and then indirectly in the soul. In the Spirit-love it was Mary's soul that was first ravished, and then, not by human love, but by God. The love of God so inflamed her heart, her body, her soul, that when Jesus was born the whole world could truly say of Him, 'This is a Child of love.' As Chesterton put it:

> *That Christ from this created purity*
> *Came forth your sterile appetites to scorn.*
> *Lo! In her house Life without lust was born*
> *So in your house lust without Life shall die.*"

"Graciously receive our gifts, O Lord, as Thou wast pleased to accept the offerings of Thy high priest Melchisedech."

    —From the Roman Canon of the Holy Mass

The hands of Archbishop Fulton John Sheen as cast in a sculpture by the New York artist Ray Shaw.

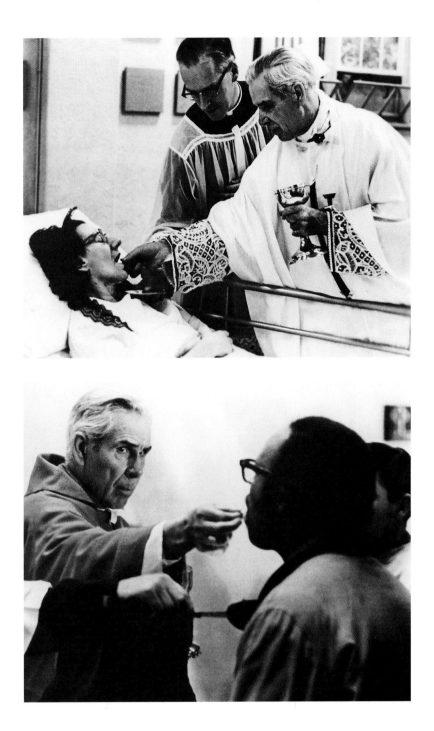

"The Eucharist is so essential to our one-ness with Christ."

Bishop Sheen officiated at the First Communion and Confirmation of Marie-Christine, the Princess of Belgium, on May 9, 1962. The larger photo shows the Bishop talking to the Princess about the importance of the sacraments.
RIGHT: *In front of the Church of Saint Joseph, in Belgium.*

"A vocation then is a falling in love with God, but it is a fall which is the prelude to a resurrection. In human love there is the meeting of two poverties; in a vocation there is a meeting of the poverty of self and the riches of God. Such love becomes an eternal flame ignited from the Heavenly Fire Which is God."

—From a 1952 article entitled "Psychology of Vocations for the Young".

"God is not something that is acquired only at the end of a reasoning process. He is Someone to Whom we respond, as a child responds to a father's love."

"It is not we who prove God; it is God Who 'proves us', in the sense that He searches out our ways: 'Lord, Thou hast searched me out and known me.' "

"Communism is a religion, a surrender to the absolute. That is why it appeals to those who are without faith."

Monsignor Sheen on the steps of the Nanking Cathedral on his trip to China in April 1948.

"The therapeutic for our vaulting pride is reliance and trust in God. There are here two extremes to be avoided: one is to believe that man does everything and God does nothing, which is the Western sin of pride. The other is to believe that God does everything and man does nothing, which is the Oriental sin of fatalism."

—From a newspaper column by Bishop Sheen.

Then (first Catholic) Governor Al Smith of New York and Fulton J. Sheen were good friends over the years and spent considerable time together.

TOP: *Al Smith, Father Sheen, and Cardinal Hayes of New York.*
BOTTOM: *Bishop Sheen on a golf outing with Al Smith (far right).*

"Each man, therefore, is to a great extent the creature of his own world, and the solution he brings to the world's problems will, to a great extent, depend upon his own inner condition. It will be found that those who lack a moral character will almost always find the fault in external environment."

TOP: *Monsignor Sheen at the head table, with Al Smith to his left. Cardinal Spellman is at the far left end of the table.*

BOTTOM: *At Cliff Haven, New York, summer of 1937; to the left of Monsignor Sheen is Al Smith, and to Monsignor Sheen's right is George Gillespie. To the left of Al Smith is Monsignor Michael Splaine of Boston, president of the Catholic Summer School.*

"In becoming the Mother of men, Mary also became 'the spouse of Christ'. So Christ and His Mother brought forth at the cross their spiritual progeny, which we are. She is our Mother, not by title of courtesy; she is our Mother because she endured at that particular moment the pains of childbirth for all of us . . ."

LEFT: *Bishop Sheen with Bishop O'Meara in front of the Basilica at Lourdes, France.*

RIGHT: *The Bishop filling a container of the Lourdes water to bring back home.*

"And why did Our Lord give her to us as Mother? Because He knew we could never be holy without her. He came to us through her purity, and only through her purity can we go back to her. There is no Sanctus apart from Mary. Every victim who mounts that altar under the species of bread and wine must have said the Confiteor and become a holy victim—but there is no holiness without Mary."

—From a 1936 radio broadcast entitled "Mary Was 'Willed' to Us by Our Lord."

LEFT: *Bishop Sheen offering Holy Mass at one of the indoor shrines at Lourdes.*
RIGHT: *Bishop Sheen offering Holy Mass at the outside shrine at Lourdes.*

HIS MOTHER IS THE KEY

Our Lord had only a foster father, but He had a real mother. It was she who gave to Him His human life— gave Him Hands with which to bless children; Feet with which to go in search of stray sheep; Eyes with which to weep over dead friends and a corrupt civilization; and a Body with which He might suffer. It was through this Mother that He became the Bridge between the divine and the human. If we take her away, then either God does not become Man, or he that is born of her is a man, and not God. Without her we would no longer have Our Lord.

If we have a box in which we keep our money, we know the one thing we must always give attention to is the key; we never think that the key is the money, but we know that without the key we cannot get into our money. The Mother of the Babe is like that key; without her we cannot get to Our Lord because He came through her. She is not to be compared to Our Lord, for she is a creature and He is the Creator. But without her we could not understand how the Bridge was built between heaven and earth.

As she formed Jesus in her body, so she forms Jesus in our souls. In this one Woman, virginity and motherhood are united, as if God willed to show that both are necessary for the world. Those things which are separated in other creatures are united in her. The Mother is the protector of the Virgin and the Virgin is also the inspiration of Motherhood.

"All of you who have lain crucified on beds of pain, remember that an hour will come when you will be taken down from your cross, and the Savior shall look upon your hands and feet and sides to find there the imprint of His wounds, which will be your passport to Eternal Joy."

"There are two kinds of freedom; one is freedom *from* something, the other is freedom *for* something. One is freedom of choice which enables us to choose between good and evil; the other is the higher freedom which rests in the attainment of truth and goodness."

Bishop Sheen speaking at an unidentified military commemoration, July 1970.

TOP: *Monsignor Sheen is greeted by commanding officers at the Pentagon.*
BOTTOM: *In June 1948, Monsignor Sheen arrived in Japan and was introduced to Miss E. V. Alexander, head of the Visitors Bureau of the general's headquarters at the Imperial Hotel in Tokyo, and Colonel J. S. Harbison on behalf of General Douglas MacArthur.*

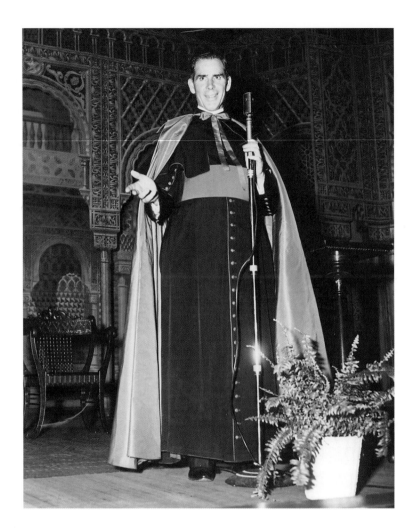

"Speaking on 'The Way, the Truth, and the Life', [Monsignor Sheen] asserted that Christ is 'unique in the religious history of the world and as different from all other teachers and reformers as God is different from men', because He is identical with the truths He taught. There was no ideal outside the historical life of Christ, because 'He is the Ideal.' There was no system outside His Person. His Person is the system. There is no way apart from His Way, no truth apart from His Truth, no life apart from His Life. There is nothing outside Him or beyond Him, for in Him all the scattered ways and truths and lives find their center and source."

—From a 1930s newspaper article commenting on a Sheen radio broadcast.

"The Church will not be rescued from the present crisis by the bishops, priests, and religious, but by the laity."

At the 1940 commencement at the University of Notre Dame, Monsignor Sheen addressed the graduating class at the baccalaureate ceremonies. From left: Reverend Hugh O'Donnell, C.S.C., president of the university, Monsignor Sheen, Joseph P. Kennedy, who gave the commencement address and received an honorary doctor of laws degree, and Monsignor Michael J. Ready, S.T.D., secretary of the National Catholic Welfare Conference.

"The [Second] Vatican Council was held at that period of history when it was necessary to strike a balance between two extremes both in the world and in the Church: individualism and socialism. By individualism I mean the emphasis on the right of the individual either to develop his own spirituality or economically to increase his own capital without much concern for the social good. By socialism I mean the stress on social welfare with little concern for either the individual's religion or his morals."

Bishop Sheen seen inside Saint Peter's Basilica during the Second Vatican Council.

Bishop Sheen in attendance at the sessions of the Second Vatican Council.

LEFT: *Conferring with another bishop in Vatican City.*
RIGHT: *Seated in the tiers within Saint Peter's.*

"To My Dear Friends, the Waitresses:
"You call it a spiritual bouquet, but to me it is a garden—a veritable
spiritual Eden. You humbly sign yourselves 'The Waitresses', i.e., ladies
who serve. I am immediately reminded of Him Who also said, 'I came not
to be ministered unto but to minister.' In heaven those whom you now
serve will serve you. I am deeply grateful to each of you, and I only wish I
had arranged a special talk for you. But that my thanks may not be empty
I shall offer Mass for your intention tomorrow morning. God love you. I
am going to sign myself 'The Waiter', for I too must serve—serve you,
serve the world, serve the cause of Christ. Then as 'Waiter and Waitresses'
we shall march together to the Table of the King, where is spread the
Everlasting Banquet."

—From a newspaper story dated July 29, 1939, reporting on an occasion
when some forty waitresses heard Monsignor Sheen speak. They were so
impressed with him, they offered him a spiritual bouquet.

"When the compassionate Lord appears at Easter in the newness of life, He says to man: 'Love is stronger than death. I now appear to you so that you may be guiltless if you trust in Me. No one can accuse you of the deicide, for there is no longer a corpse to condemn you, but only a living Love to pardon you.' This is Easter. If the guilty man allows this irruption of pardon and reconciliation into his heart, he becomes a new man, whether he wears new clothes or not."

—From a newspaper column by Bishop Sheen.

Archbishop Sheen was the keynote speaker at the Holy Year Rally on September 7, 1975, in New Orleans, Louisiana.

"Trust Him when dark doubts assail thee;
Trust Him when trust is small.
Trust Him when simply to trust Him
Is the hardest thing of all."

"Men too often play with opportunity as a toy, and when their eyes are opened to see its value, lo! it has vanished. Many reach the margin of a glorious destiny and then turn back to the desert."

—From a newspaper column by Bishop Sheen.

"Inside truth is honesty; that is why in certain flashes of our real nature, we feel awkward, ashamed and haunted by our meanness, our brutality, and our selfishness. Sometimes other people get inside us and we react: 'That person gets on my nerves.' It is when we reach that point where we say that of ourselves that we have the true estimate of our worth."

—From a newspaper column by Bishop Sheen.

"If we forget the moral and the religious, what standard of right have we? The only standard of right left in democracy is the majority, and thus we would conform our democracy into an arithmocracy. Wrong is wrong, even if everybody is wrong."

Bishop Sheen with Pope Paul VI. It was Paul VI who appointed him Bishop of Rochester, New York, and later bestowed on him the title of Archbishop of the Titular See, Newport (Wales), in 1969.

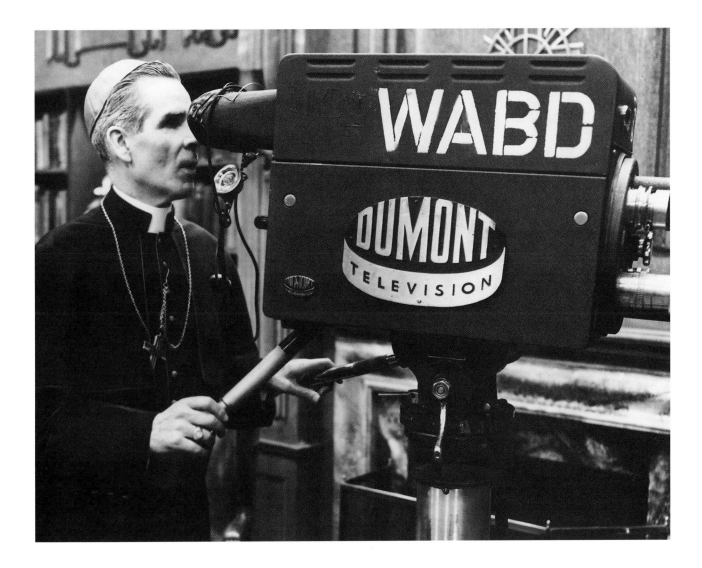

"Our era has been misnamed the 'atomic age'; it is rather the 'television age'. Television influences human brains a thousand times more than the fission and the fusion of atoms. Television is the newborn babe of the Fourth Dimension of Space-Time. Newton knocked the boundaries out of space; Einstein knocked the boundaries out of time, but television has annihilated space and time."

TOP LEFT: *Monsignor Sheen, upon his visit to Fort Bragg, is entertained by the 9th Division Band.*

TOP RIGHT: *With Father Cahill, chaplain of the "Rugged" 36th Engineers, Fort Bragg.*

BOTTOM LEFT: *Members of the 36th Engineers greeting Monsignor Sheen.*

BOTTOM RIGHT: *Monsignor Sheen with Catholic military chaplains.*

"The Irishman lives in a bigger world than Ireland, he climbs bigger hills than Killarney, he knows of deeper waters than the Shannon, and of harder rocks than Blarney. He is, in fact, always drawing upon a greater reservoir of humor than any other man on earth. He takes his jokes from a bigger book, which happens to be the book of eternity; and that is why he always talks about angels, witches, ghosts, leprechauns, shoemaker fairies, banshees, and a thousand and one other spirits that do not belong to this world, but the next."

—From the Friendly Sons of Saint Patrick banquet, Astor Hotel, New York City, March 17, 1931.

LEFT: *Bishop Sheen emerging from old Saint Patrick's Church in Chicago after the annual Saint Patrick's Day Mass in 1976.*
RIGHT: *Bishop Sheen with John Cardinal Cody, Archbishop of Chicago. The Bishop spoke at the Conrad Hilton later that night for the Sons of Erin Banquet.*

"It is not of great moment to be constantly asking ourselves if we love our neighbor. What is important is to act out that love. We learn to walk by walking, to play by playing and to love by loving. If we do anybody whom we hate a good turn, we find that we hate him less; if we do him an evil turn, we discover that we hate him more. Doing kind acts to people makes us find all people lovable. And if love is not there, we put it there and then everyone becomes lovable."

Bishop Sheen visiting the Saint Joseph's House of Hospitality, Rochester, New York, 1957.

"To a great extent the level of any civilization is the level of its womanhood. When a man loves a woman, he has to become worthy of her. The higher her virtue, the more noble her character, the more devoted she is to truth, justice, and goodness, the more a man has to aspire to be worthy of her. The history of civilization could actually be written in terms of the *level of its women*."

Members of Saint Bartholomew's Episcopal Church in New York City greet Archbishop Sheen, who was invited to be their guest speaker during Lent.

"Miss no single opportunity of making some small sacrifice, here by a smiling look, there by a kindly word; always doing the smallest thing right and doing it all for love."

— Saint Thérèse of Lisieux

Bishop Sheen speaking on an anniversary celebration of Saint Thérèse of Lisieux.

"The reason why there is a degeneration in the moral order and a decay of decency is because men and women have lost the higher love. Ignoring Christ their Saviour, Who loved them unto Calvary, and Mary, who loved them unto becoming Queen of Martyrs beneath that Cross, they have nothing for which to make the sacrifice. The only way love can be shown in this world is by sacrifice, namely, the surrender of one thing for another."

—From a radio address on March 13, 1939, for *The Catholic Hour.*

Archbishop Sheen addressing some fifteen hundred delegates and guests at the opening meeting of the Supreme Council of the Knights of Columbus in Miami Beach, Florida, in August 1975.

"When the Church is holy, dissension is from the outside; when the Church is unholy, dissension is from within."

Bishop Sheen with Francis Cardinal Spellman. Archbishop Sheen served as an auxiliary bishop of New York City prior to becoming the bishop of Rochester, New York.

"I knew that if I should leave this earth, I would be with Christ; if I remained, Christ would be here too."

Archbishop Sheen leaving New York's Lenox Hill Hospital after his open-heart surgery in 1977. On his left is Dr. Eugene Walsh, chief of the surgical team, and on his right, Dr. Michael Bruno, the Archbishop's personal physician.

"If civilization is to return to the Father's house, if the world is to be saved, it must, like the prodigal son, realize that there is such a thing as sin, and cry out from the depths of its soul, 'I have sinned.' The world today is not living in heresy, but in paganism, for it denies the whole truth of Christianity, and if the Church is to assist in the return of civilization to the Father's house the Church must come out of the catacombs to fight paganism as she did in the first century."

—From the concluding sermon in his Lenten series at Saint Patrick's Cathedral, March 24, 1934.

TOP: *In 1974, Archbishop Sheen received the Morality in Media Award at a dinner in New York City. To his left are Father Morton A. Hill, S.J., Rabbi Julius Neumann, and New York Fire Commissioner John T. O'Hagan.*
BOTTOM: *The Archbishop with Bud Wilkinson, former Oklahoma football coach, at the thirty-third Interreligious National Bible Week luncheon, in New York City.*

Bishop Sheen in Rochester, New York, in 1969, at a reception for the fiftieth anniversary of his ordination to the priesthood.

"Sit down quickly and write fifty"—LUKE 16:16

The twentieth day of September, nineteen sixty-nine,
Thanks to the mercies of the Good Lord,
I am a priest for fifty years.
No celebration marks the anniversary except your prayers
And my own silent thanksgiving in a Trappist Monastery.
You know why: Any good done in these five decades
Was because God held my hand.

> "What do you have that was not given to you?
> And if it was given, how can you boast as if it were your own?"
> (I COR 4:7)

Only the worthless things are mine, when my ego walked alone.
If it be a terrible thing to fall into the hands of the Living God,
It is a more terrible thing to fall out of them.

IN RETROSPECT

In that scroll and sequence of years, for what am I most thankful?
First, when born, my mother, like Hannah,
Laid me on the altar of the Blessed Mother
And dedicated me to the service of her Son.
This is my blessed assurance that the Lord will one day say,
"I heard My Mother speak of you."

Second, that each morn at Holy Mass,
I could hear drifting from a Cross:
"Can you drink My Cup?"
"Can you watch an hour?"

Third, thanks, dear Lord, for suffering to see that
Not all the crosses are on hills.
"Dragged like a plowshare through the heart,
Only new furrows cause the grain to start."

This text is from the program for the fiftieth anniversary of Bishop Sheen's ordination to the priesthood.

Fourth, as bishop, I might, as head
Feel the pain of every member of the Body.

And as a weak cell of that Body,
Sense unity with brother priests
Who love that head whose name is Peter.

Fifth, my thanks for our *Presbyterium*,
For my brothers of Bread and Cup
Who have met with me in shared griefs and joys
And daily restored the spiritual fortune of the diocese,
As "God restored Job's fortune because he prayed for his friends."
    (JOB 42:10)

IN PROSPECT

What do I see and hope?
I see the Lord cleaning house,
Testing the Church as He did the Germans with Nazism,
The Russians with Communism,
And us with worldliness and half-drawn blades.

I see the few who lose their way
But, thank God, because they never throw away the map,
One day will come home again.

I see that though the doubters have choked the spiritual life,
As the Philistines choked the wells of Abraham,
Yet, if we but dig, as Isaac did,
We will find the underground waters of Life
Still there, buried and undestroyed.

I see the role of the priest has not changed.
Astronauts are not different persons on the moon—
Only their milieu changes;
If they carried not their atmosphere with them,
They would perish, as would we priests
Without the "sweet odor of Christ".

I see that if Secular Man turns us off,
It is because we give him only paperback sociology,
And not the *Theology of the Crucified.*
The doubting world, like Thomas, will believe
Only when we too show the red scars of Love.

I see that we must not dig holes
Until we have something to build therein:
That if our scalpels are poisoned with hate,
We can bring no healing to broken wings.
That though some may tear at Mother Church's flesh,
Yet not one bone of that Body will ever be broken.

I see that fifty years ago, we were wrong in saying:
"The Word became flesh and dwelt amongst us
Churchgoers, the respectable, the good and the white."
And I see that we are wrong today in changing the tune:
"The World became flesh and dwelt among the
Rebels, the blacks, and the protesters."
We will be right again when we believe
God is the Father of all men,
And so show Christ to Negroes that they will see Him black,
And they will so show Him to us, that we will see Him white.

I see a rebirth of a priesthood
That will love the poor, without hating the rich,
That will serve the Church not despising those who bear its agonies,
And whose every dialogue will begin by a monologue before God.

I see the more we priests love, the more we will suffer,
As the distraught father suffers more than the delinquent son.
But our suffering love will take the worst this world can offer,
And press it as another drop in the chalice of Redemption.

I see that our gravity is too earthly—
We are weighted with prayerless days.
Oh! to trust our weight on the Weightless Spirit
And step out like astronauts on the shelf of Grace
And not fall,
As Christ holds our hand.

CONCLUSION

My work, please the Lord, is not finished.
Much is still to be done, while there is light.
Non recuso laborem.
To close the generation gap,

Each day I will say:
"I will go to the altar of God, to God Who renews my youth."

The Lord did not begin to preach Wisdom and the Cross
Until He was over thirty.
So I await His Promise to those planted in the House of God:
    "They will bear fruit in old age,
      Still remaining fresh and green."—PSALMS 92:14

As I work under the aegis of two hearts—
One Sacred and the other Immaculate,
I will sing with Hammarskjold:

        "The road,
        I shall follow it.

        The fun,
        I shall forget it.

        The cup,
        I shall empty it.

        The pain,
        I shall conceal it.

        The truth,
        I shall be told it.

        The end,
        I shall endure it.

+ FULTON J. SHEEN

"You have written and spoken well of the Lord Jesus. You are a loyal son of the Church."

—Pope John Paul II to Archbishop Sheen

His Holiness John Paul II exchanges the kiss of peace inside Saint Patrick's Cathedral, New York City, October 2, 1979, on his first visit to the United States as pope.

FULTON JOHN SHEEN

May 8, 1895 — December 9, 1979

HOMILY

DELIVERED AT THE FUNERAL LITURGY
OF
ARCHBISHOP FULTON J. SHEEN
BY
ARCHBISHOP EDWARD T. O'MEARA, S.T.D.
NATIONAL DIRECTOR OF THE
SOCIETY FOR THE PROPAGATION OF THE FAITH
ARCHBISHOP-DESIGNATE OF INDIANAPOLIS
SAINT PATRICK'S CATHEDRAL
NEW YORK CITY
DECEMBER 13, 1979

My dear Friends:

A voice is silent in the midst of the Church and in our land, the like of which will not be heard again in our day. The vocation of Fulton Sheen is consummated: he has responded with one final "yes" to the call of God—a "yes" so final that human frailty and infirmity can never reverse it.

On September the twentieth of this year, with five of his friends, I listened to Archbishop Sheen review his life during the celebration of the Eucharist which was his thanksgiving to God for sixty years in the priesthood. His own division of his life into three periods will serve us well on this occasion.

First there was the vocation, the call from God, that was as clear to him as was God's call to Jeremiah the Prophet in the Old Testament passage we have just heard, and as the "come and see" of Jesus Himself to John's disciples in the Gospel passage. Never was there a time in his life when he did not want to be a priest; never was there a time in his life when he wished he had pursued another career.

Part of his response to that call from God was a practice he started in the year of his ordination to the priesthood. Every day began with the very first hour, the freshest and therefore the best hour—he was a morning person—given to God in prayer. This was his Holy Hour, and it was always made in the presence of the Blessed Sacrament. The practice continued without interruption for the next sixty years. As surely as we are here in Saint Patrick's Cathedral this afternoon, he made his Holy Hour last Sunday morning, the day of his passing.

Whenever he chose to respond to those who asked him the secret of his ability to touch minds and hearts, his answer was always—"the Holy Hour"—when he spoke to God, and listened to God speaking to him. Here his conflicts were reconciled, for he held no opinions lightly; here his anxieties and insecurities were calmed, for he was the most human of men; here his heart was literally set on fire with the drive that made him ever restless to respond totally to God's call.

This period of his life marked also the expanding of his intellect and the growth of his constant pursuit of excellence and quality. He used to say frequently how grateful he was to the Church for the marvelous education he received, which opened his mind to an intellectual curiosity that never deserted him. He always had to have new books; he loved meeting interesting and informed people; the latest scientific discoveries and technological devices fascinated him.

On the twentieth of September, Archbishop Sheen spoke of the second period of his life as the Period of Proclamation. Returning from Europe in 1925, the amazing career of oratory, teaching, and preaching began. He was the first to have an on-going series of religious radio broadcasts, the first churchman to have a regular television program. The pulpit of this great Cathedral became his over the years as throngs came to hear his sermons, and therein lies the touchingly beautiful significance of his burial in the vault under the High Altar. His pen produced over sixty books, as well as articles and letters that will never be numbered. Always he addressed himself to the thought of the times, and insisted that a speaker must begin his message from where his hearers are, not where he is.

It was during this time of his life that the Church asked him to direct the Society for the Propagation of the Faith in the United States. By that time his reputation was solidly established as a Professor at the Catholic University of America. Many asked him how he could leave such a position for this seemingly narrower apostolate . . . to which he replied: "I have pushed out the classroom walls, and now I can embrace the whole world." In this role he would be expected to intensify missionary enthusiasm within the Church and to gather financial help for missionary needs.

The Church throughout the world is his eternal debtor for the way he discharged this responsibility. He gave missionaries all over the world a new sense of the dignity of their vocation. He capsulated missionary ideals in short unforgettable phrases:

It was a pagan Latin poet who said that charity begins at home.

On a dry and rocky hillside between Jerusalem and Jericho, a certain Samaritan taught us that with Christ charity begins away from home, and with the most unattractive of our neighbors.

Again:

Our charity to the poor of the world is measured by God, not so much by what we give, but by how much we have kept for ourselves after our giving. That is why the widow's mite was such a large gift; she gave all that she had.

Again, talking to people like myself:

We can say that to dig we are not able, but let us never say that to beg we are ashamed.

His love for the Society for the Propagation of the Faith endured in life and in death, and surely you are not surprised that both in life and in death he gave it his every earthly possession.

Many came to faith in Christ and the Church through his words, and for every famous name he instructed, there were hundreds of others who were just as important to him as those in the public eye. His presentation of the fullness of the Catholic faith was powerful and convincing. One of his converts spoke for all of them and summed up this gift of his at the finish of an instruction by leaping to her feet and, with clenched fists, shouting heavenward: "O, God, what a protagonist you have in this man!"

On the twentieth of September, Archbishop Sheen spoke also of a third period in his life. It was the one wherein he began to know Christ as never before, to love Him with ever greater intensity, and to experience unspeakable peace. In retrospect, this period seemed to me to begin with the writing of his monumental *Life of Christ* in the late 1950s. Gradually he divested himself of his possessions; he was a man who loved beautiful things. But they became less and less important to him as Christ became more and more important, and as his comprehension of the mystery of the Cross increased.

Frequently he spoke of his death to the amazement and oftentimes the consternation of his hearers and friends. But he said: "It is not that I do not love life; I do. It is just that I want to see the Lord. I have spent hours before Him in the Blessed Sacrament. I have spoken to Him in prayer, and about Him to everyone who would listen, and now I want to see Him face to face."

If we could ask him now, I am sure he would say that the apex of his career took place here in the Sanctuary of Saint Patrick's Cathedral on this year's

October second, when Pope John Paul II enveloped him in a brotherly embrace. Later, I asked him what the Holy Father said as the two stood there. "He told me that I had written and spoken well of the Lord Jesus, and that I was a loyal son of the Church."

Last Sunday at 7:15 P.M., God called Archbishop Fulton Sheen to Himself by name. It was a moment known to God, and fixed by Him from all eternity, a call to perfect life and truth and love, a call to a life he will never tire of, that can never be improved, and which he can never lose.

Dear Friend, Archbishop Sheen, we are all better because you were in our midst and were our friend. We trust you to the care of your "Lovely Lady dressed in blue". We pray that Jesus has already said: "I've heard My Mother speak of you."

Bye now, Fulton Sheen, and God Love You Forever!

IN RETROSPECT

In that scroll and sequence of years, for what am I most thankful?
First, when born, my mother, like Hannah,
Laid me on the altar of the Blessed Mother
And dedicated me to the service of her Son.
This is my blessed assurance that the Lord will one day say,
"I heard My Mother speak of you."

Fulton J. Sheen

CHRONOLOGY

BASIC INFORMATION

Born El Paso, Illinois, May 8, 1895
Ordained, September 20, 1919
Papal Chamberlain, 1934
Domestic Prelate, 1935
National Director, SPOF, 1950–1966
Appointed Bishop by Pius XII, 1951
Auxiliary Bishop of New York, 1951–1966
Appointed to Vatican Council II, Commission on the Missions, by Pope John XXIII, 1962
Appointed to post-conciliar Commission on the Missions by Pope Paul VI, 1965
Consecrated missionary bishops with Pope John XXIII in St Peter's, Rome, May 1960 and May 1961
Appointed Bishop of Rochester, New York, by Pope Paul VI, 1966
Elected by the American Episcopacy Chairman of Committee for the Propagation of the Faith, 1966
Elected by the American Episcopacy to the Administrative Board of the National Council of Catholic Bishops, 1966
Appointed to the Papal Commission for Non-Believers by Pope Paul VI, 1969
Named Archbishop of the Titular See of Newport (Wales) by Pope Paul VI, 1969
Named Assistant at the Pontifical Throne by Pope Paul VI, July 1976
Died in the Lord, New York City, December 9, 1979

ACADEMIC DEGREES

J.C.B., Catholic University of America, 1920
Ph.D., Louvain, Belgium, 1923
S.T.D., Rome, 1924
Agrégé en philosophie, Louvain, 1925
Honorary: LL.D., Litt.D., L.H.D.

EDUCATOR

Dogmatic theology professor, St. Edmund's College, Ware, England, 1925
Philosophy professor, Catholic University of America, 1926–1950

PREACHER

Summer Conferences, Westminster, London, 1925, 1928, 1931
Catholic Summer School, Cambridge University, 1930, 1931
Annual Broadcasts, *The Catholic Hour*, 1930–1952

BOOKS

Christian Order and the Family
Holy Hour Readings and Prayers for a Daily Holy Hour
What I Can Do
God and Intelligence in Modern Philosophy, 1925
Religion without God, 1928
The Life of All Living, 1929 (revised 1979)
Communism Answers Questions of a Communist, 1930
The Divine Romance, 1930
Old Errors and New Labels, 1931
The Church and the Times, 1932
Manifestations of Christ, 1932
Moods and Truths, 1932
The Way of the Cross, 1932
Hymn of the Conquered, 1933
The Seven Last Words, 1933
The Eternal Galilean, 1934
The Philosophy of Science, 1934
Call to Catholic Action, 1935
The Fullness of Christ, 1935
The Mystical Body of Christ, 1935
Calvary and the Mass, 1936
Liberty under Communism, 1936
The Moral Universe, 1936
Freedom and Democracy: A Study of Their Enemies, 1937
The Cross and the Beatitudes, 1937
Justice and Charity, 1938
Liberty, Equality, and Fraternity, 1938
Patriotism, 1938
The Cross and the Crisis, 1938
The Rainbow of Sorrow, 1938
Victory over Vice, 1939
Challenge to Charity, 1940
Freedom under God, 1940
Peace the Fruit of Justice, 1940
Prayer Book for Our Times, 1940
The Seven Virtues, 1940
Universal Norm of Morality, 1940
Whence Wars Come, 1940
A Declaration of Dependence, 1941
Conditions of a Just War, 1941
For God and Country, 1941
The Cross and the Double Cross, 1941
What Are We Fighting For, 1941
God and War and Peace, 1942
Keeping the Faith with God in America, 1942
Two Swords, 1942
What the War Teaches Us about Salvation, 1942
Philosophies at War, 1943
Shield of Faith, 1943
The Armor of God, 1943
The Divine Verdict, 1943
Love One Another, 1944
Seven Pillars of Peace, 1944
Seven Words to the Cross, 1944
Seven Words of Jesus and Mary, 1945
The Seventh Word, 1945
Life and the Kingdom of Jesus in Christian, 1946
Love on Pilgrimage, 1946
Preface to Religion, 1946
Jesus, Son of Mary, 1947
You, 1947
Communism and the Conscience of the West, 1948
The Modern Soul in Search of God, 1948
The Philosophy of Religion: The Impact of Modern Knowledge on Religion, 1948
Peace of Soul, 1949
Lift Up Your Heart, 1950
Rock Plunged into Eternity, 1950
Love That Waits for You, 1951
Three to Get Married, 1951
Crisis in Christendom, 1952
Crisis in History, 1952
Meditations on the 15 Mysteries of the Rosary, 1952
The Prodigal World, 1952
The World's First Love, 1952
Characters of the Passion, 1953
Life Is Worth Living, vol. 1, 1953
Life Is Worth Living, vol. 2, 1954
The Church, Communism, and Democracy, 1954
The Life of Christ, 1954
Way to Happiness, 1954
Way to Inner Peace, 1954
God Loves You, 1955
Life Is Worth Living, vol. 3, 1955
Thinking Life Through, 1955
Thoughts for Daily Living, 1955
Life Is Worth Living, vol. 4, 1956
Ideological Fallacies of Communism, 1957
Life Is Worth Living, vol. 5, 1957
Life of Christ, 1958 (revised 1977)
This Is the Mass, 1958 (revised 1965)
Go to Heaven, 1960
This Is Rome, 1960
This Is the Holy Land, 1961
These Are the Sacraments, 1962
Choice: The Sacred or Profane Life, 1963
Church of the Poor, 1963
Message to the Catholics of the United States, 1963
The Priest Is Not His Own, 1963
Missions and the World Crisis, 1964
The Power of Love, 1965
Walk with God, 1965
Christmas Inspirations, 1966
Footprints in a Darkened Forest, 1966 [or 1967]
Easter Inspirations, 1967
Guide to Contentment, 1967
That Tremendous Love, 1967
The Quotable Fulton J. Sheen, 1967
Wit and Wisdom of Bishop Fulton J. Sheen, 1969
Children and Parents, 1970
Those Mysterious Priests, 1974
Life Is Worth Living, 1st and 2nd series, 1978, abridged
Treasure in Clay: The Autobiography of Fulton J. Sheen, 1980
On Being Human, 1982
The Last Seven Words, 1982
Cross Ways: A Book of Inspiration, 1984
Rejoice, 1984

TO OUR LADY

Lovely Lady dressed in blue—
Teach me how to pray!
God was just your little boy,
Tell me what to say!

Did you lift Him up, sometimes,
Gently on your knee?
Did you sing to Him the way
Mother does to me?

Did you hold His hand at night?
Did you ever try
Telling Him stories of the world?
O! And did He cry?

Do you really think He cares
If I tell him things—
Little things that happen? And
Do the Angel's Wings

Make a noise? And can He hear
Me if I speak low?
Does He understand me now?
Tell me—for you know!

Lovely Lady dressed in blue—
Teach me how to pray!
God was just your little boy—
And you know the way!

Bishop Sheen's favorite poem.

Reprinted with the permission of Macmillan Publishing Co., Inc.
from *The Child on His Knees* by Mary Dixon Thayer.
Copyright © 1926 by Macmillan Publishing Co., Inc.,
renewed 1954 by Mary D. T. Fremont-Smith

PHOTOGRAPH CREDITS

Editor's note: all photographs are under the auspices of Saint Bernard's Institute, to which the late Archbishop Fulton J. Sheen left them to their perpetual care. The initials SBI refer to Saint Bernard's Institute. All efforts have been made to identify the sources of the photos used. Our apologies to those whose credit should appear but for whom no contacts were provided on the back of the photos.

2, WFJ Ryan; 3, SBI; 4, WFJ Ryan; 5, Archdiocese of Indianapolis; 10, SBI; 9, SBI; Society for the Propagation of the Faith; 12, SBI; 15, SBI; 16, D. J. Zehnder; 17, SBI; 18, SBI; 19, SBI; 20, Wm. Lavendar; 21, Wm. Lavendar; 22, SBI; 23, SBI; 24, SBI; 25, SBI; 26, Boutrelle; 27, Boutrelle; 28, Joseph Sheen (The Chicago Editorial Office); 29, SBI; 30, SBI; 31, Louis C. Assad; 32, SBI; 33, SBI; 34, Y. Tourigny, Society for the Propagation of the Faith; 35, Archdiocese of Indianapolis; 37, T. Gordon Massecar; 38, Religious News Service; 39, A. Polasek; 40, SBI; 41, M. Boris; 42, SBI; 43, John Wright; 44, SBI; 45, Associated Press; 47, E. Foley; 48, SBI; 49, Hessler Studio; 51, SBI; 52, Associated Press, SBI; 53, G. Felici, United Press International; 55, Ernest Amato, Louis Preuzer; 56, Marcelo Fortunato, SBI; 57, Religious News Service, SBI, Marcelo Fortunato; 58, SBI; 59, SBI; 60, SBI; 61, SBI; 62, Associated Press, SBI, Belaga, SBI; 63, M. Boris, SBI; 64, G. Felici, Archdiocese of Indianapolis; 65, G. Felici, Archdiocese of Indianapolis; 66, SBI; 67, *Catholic Chronicle*; 68, SBI; 69, SBI; 70, SBI; 71, SBI; 72, SBI; 73, SBI; 74, SBI; 75, Eric Ventur, Australia Department of Information; 77, *Palm Beach Register*; 78, SBI; 79, Louis Ouzer; 80–81, Bill Mason, Crystal Cathedral; 82, SBI; 83, Archdiocese of Indianapolis; 84, SBI; 85, G. Felici, Foto-Rome, Archdiocese of Indianapolis; 86, Religious News Service, SBI; 87, SBI; 88, Religious News Service; 89, Archdiocese of Indianapolis, SBI; 90, SBI; 92, SBI; 93, Religious News Service; 94, Belga, SBI; 95, National Catholic photos, SBI; 96, Ernest Amato; 97, SBI; 98, SBI; 99, Morgan Photo; 100, SBI; 101, SBI; 102, Lacaze, Archdiocese of Indianapolis; 103, Archdiocese of Indianapolis, SBI; 105, SBI; 106, SBI; 107, Nutter, SBI; 108, SBI; 109, SBI; 110, G. Felici, Archdiocese of Indianapolis; 111, G. Felici, Archdiocese of Indianapolis; 112, Peppy's Photos; 113, SBI; 114, SBI; 115, SBI; 116, SBI; 117, Boris, SBI; 118, SBI; 119, Archdiocese of Indianapolis; 120, SBI; 121, George Quinn, SBI; 122, E. Foley; 123, SBI; 124, SBI; 125, Knights of Columbus Archives; 126, SBI; 127, Religious News Service, SBI; 128, James Hefferman; 129, Religious News Service; 130, SBI; 131, M. Boris; 132, SBI; 133, SBI; 134, SBI; 135, SBI; 136, E. Foley; 141, Edda Taylor.